Boogie Woogie for Beginners

A Piano Method by Frank Paparelli

ISBN 978-0-634-09347-0

HAL•LEONARD®
CORPORATION
7777 W. BLUEMOUND RD. P.O. BOX 13819 MILWAUKEE, WI 53213

Visit Hal Leonard Online at
www.halleonard.com

Chapter One

THE BOOGIE WOOGIE STYLE

What is Boogie Woogie

Boogie Woogie is a twelve-measure Jazz form with a unique rhythm in the bass. The bass features a repeating figure which for the most part takes the form of eight eighth notes to the measure.

It is from its almost characteristic use of an eight-to-the-bar bass figure that Boogie Woogie is sometimes referred to as "*Eight to the Bar*".

Lift

Boogie Woogie, like all Jazz, is in 4/4 time. And all Jazz has a "lift" (resulting from the rhythm of Jazz syncopations against a steady beat.) The Boogie Woogie bass being "eight to the bar", makes for a "lift" all its own. It can have the light lift of Pine-top's *Boogie Woogie Blues*, the crashing drive of Meade Lux Lewis's *Six Wheel Chaser*, or the "jump" of Pete Johnson's *Death Ray Boogie*. One cannot limit Boogie Woogie to a specific lift or tempo. As long as the bass figure repeats itself rhythmically within the twelve-measure form, it's Boogie Woogie.

Color and Effects

Boogie Woogie is an intimate personal expression, very rich in "effects" such as rhythm, color, power, etc. When less conventional notes are used against this bass, the varying shades of Boogie Woogie "color" come out. Note the rhythmic force, color, and power in these chords:

From "Bass On Top" by Meade "Lux" Lewis

Boogie Woogie has no melody of its own in the sense that a popular song has a melody. It is based on a simple chord pattern consisting of twelve measures. A Boogie Woogie improvisation or composition consists of different variations based on this chord pattern.

4

Boogie Woogie chord Pattern

The pattern is built around the three fundamental chords of a scale, the I, IV, and

V . In the Key of C, the I is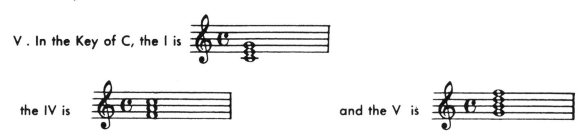

the IV is   and the V is

These chords follow each other in the sequence I, IV, I, V, I. Play this sequence on the piano and note how easily and familiarly the chords follow each other.

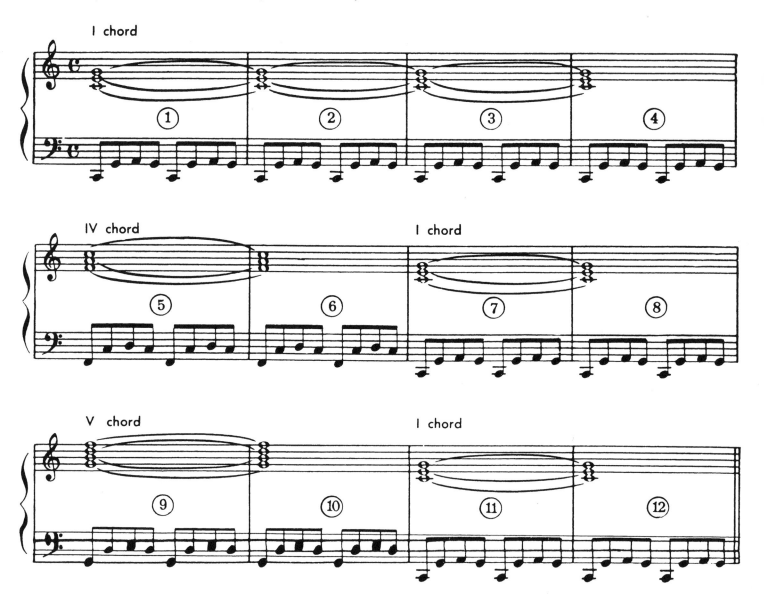

Often measures (2) and (10) change to the IV chord.

A Typical Boogie Woogie Chorus

The following is the first chorus of Pete Johnson's version of *Kaycee on My Mind*.

Medium Boogie Woogie Tempo

This chorus is rich in Boogie Woogie effects. Note the rhythm and color in the right hand. Note the syncopations in measures (4) and (10), the "tremolo" in measure (8), the off-color chords in measure (4), and the variety of sixteenth-note decorations in measures (4) (6) and (10).

Suggestions

Before you can attempt to play Boogie Woogie learn how to get the most out of listening to it.

(1) *Look at music-making as an expression, rather than simply as an attempt to create beauty.* If you have a standard conception of "good piano tone" as being "beautiful", "clinging", "sweet", etc., and apply this conception to all music—regardless of the form and expression of the music in question—get rid of this notion quickly. When you hear chords like the following,

From "Bass On Top" by Meade "Lux" Lewis

don't listen for a "beautiful" or "clinging" tone. In this passage, from Meade Lux Lewis's *Bass on Top*, the effect intended was not beauty. If the chords were held longer or played "beautifully", they would be "corny" and the original composition would be hopelessly out of taste. As a matter of fact, a "corny" rendition is one which features artificial effects—effects which the performer did not have a genuine feeling for expressing, and which he threw in tastelessly and pointlessly. This is why Jazz is so difficult for the untalented and so simple for the talented—any music which is not felt properly and is not performed in taste comes out "corny".

(2) *Do not apply any conventional "rules" of dynamics (degrees of loudness and softness) to Boogie Woogie.* The dynamics in Boogie Woogie are part of, and contained in, the original conception of ideas.

(3) *Eliminate any "rubato" (fluctuations in time) which causes the tempo to waver in Boogie Woogie.* There can be no rhythm with such a rubato. Rubato, in music other than Jazz, is frequently indulged in, and overdone by amateurs who have no sense of time and phrasing and who lack control of their hands. In Boogie Woogie the time must be strict throughout so that the rhythm (pattern of *accents in time*) can have meaning. In this connection, when you listen to Boogie Woogie do not attempt to enjoy strict time—this is quite impossible. Listen, rather, for the rhythm and "lift" resulting from the steady beat.

(4) *Try to feel at home with chromatic tones so that you won't hear them as "wrong"* notes.

From "Answer to the Prayer" by Meade "Lux" Lewis, Margaret Coleman and Bishop Edsel Ammons

If you feel these notes are "wrong" you will feel that Stravinsky, Ravel, and even Bach used "wrong" notes. In Boogie Woogie these chomatic tones must be listened to for what they are intended. At times they develop an idea, at other times, they give "color", embellish, etc.

(5) Do not use any pedals in Boogie Woogie. Pedals are almost never used in Boogie Woogie except for special tonal crashes and percussive effects which are far beyond the beginner's stage.

Chapter Two

TOUCH

How to make sound come out of a key is not the problem of playing the piano. The fundamental problem is how to play notes *consecutively in time*. If you have a system of piano-playing which reads for the most part, "don't use the arm, don't use the wrist, don't use the fingers, don't use the keys" . . . throw it out. You can never be happy under such conditions. And you certainly cannot play the piano. Playing notes consecutively in time, and with the tone desired is indeed a problem. The solution lies in relaxing and contracting the proper muscles, and in using the *least* amount of muscular exertion. As a result, any "beautiful" and "swishy" hand movements are as unnecessary and tiring at the keyboard as they are in brushing your hair. Fancy hand movements lead to lack of muscular preparation and induce fatigue and lack of control. In fact, these fancy hand-flittings are favored by the "ham" actor when he plays the role of a pianist—on a dummy piano.

Method

Don't be afraid of the piano. Do not play feebly on top of the keyboard. Play "into the keys" to acquire a firm touch.

Hit the following note:

Now, when ready, hit this note:

When ready, hit this:

The freedom with which you executed these three notes must be present at all times when you play. The following exercise is in strict time, and demands more control. Whether you are playing pp or ff, the attack on the key must be definite. Play the exercise as slowly as you wish but *be ready for each note before you play it.*

Articulation (clarity in rhythm and touch)

Play each note with the proper amount of force and hold each note precisely for the duration indicated.

Chapter Three

THE LEFT HAND

Your Boogie Woogie is only as good as your left hand. The left hand must be so mastered that it plays the bass figure automatically, naturally, solidly—without being bothered by any expression of the right hand. The left hand must be capable of playing notes consecutively in time, and it must articulate these notes in a clear rhythm. In short, it must develop endurance and control.

Single-note Bass Figure

In the following bass figure, for example, the beginner often neglects to articulate these notes.

This results in a bass figure that sounds quite different from the original figure. I have heard beginners play it this way:

This carelessness in articulation must be eliminated before the beginner acquires the habit of "sloppy" playing.

Method for practicing a bass figure

Play each note of the bass figure in a variety of graded rhythms, as indicated below.
Play only as fast as you can play with comfort, tone, and clear articulation.

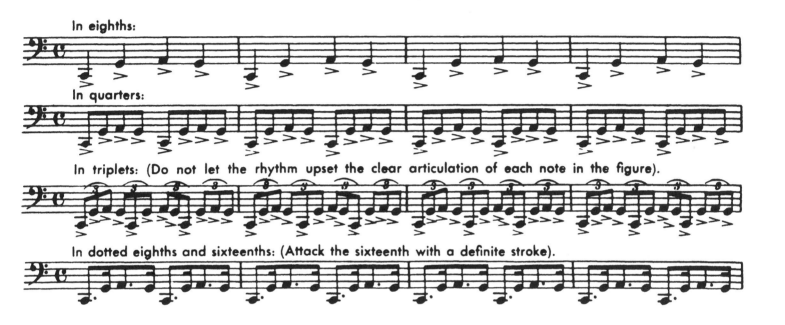

In eighths:

In quarters:

In triplets: (Do not let the rhythm upset the clear articulation of each note in the figure).

In dotted eighths and sixteenths: (Attack the sixteenth with a definite stroke).

After having studied the bass figure in these rhythms try to play the bass in the chord pattern. Each note must be even. Play in strict time and take your own tempo.

Work out a similar exercise employing the different rhythms on the following basses:

Don't be afraid of playing on black keys. Unless you become accustomed to playing on both black and white keys you cannot develop control of the keyboard.

Other types of basses

"Walking Bass"

The "walking bass" is made up of broken octaves. In the following exercise make certain the thumb articulates.

In straight eighths:

And in reverse:

In dotted eighths and sixteenths:

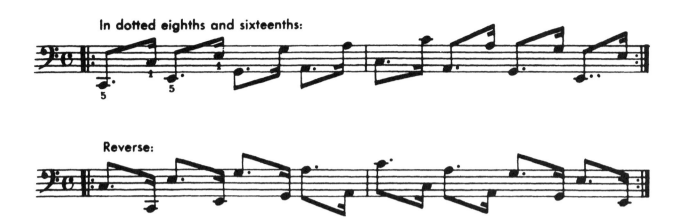

Reverse:

Play the following walking bass in the Boogie Woogie chord pattern, always at a consistent speed. When you feel you can play it faster do so, but at a consistent steady speed. After playing in eighths try it in dotted eighths and sixteenths. Don't neglect the articulation of the sixteenth notes.

In eighths:

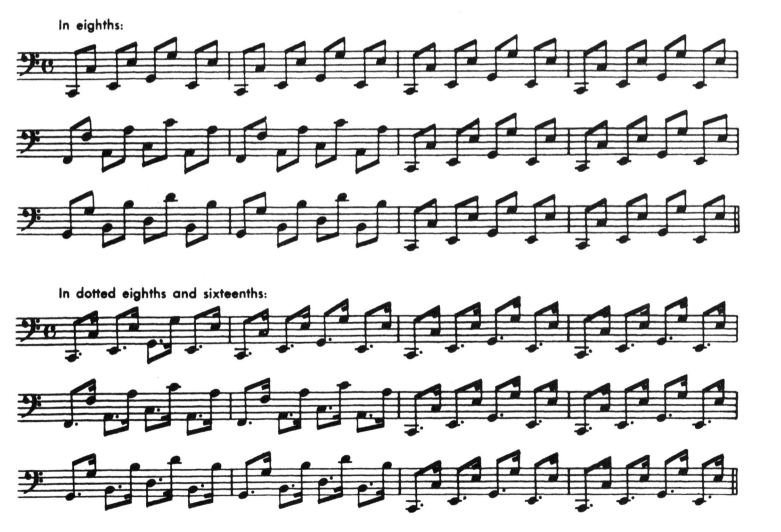

In dotted eighths and sixteenths:

Try the following different form of the walking bass. Also work it out in dotted eighths and sixteenths.

Chord Bass

Play it staccato—so that it sounds like this:

Play it in strict time til it begins to swing by itself. Don't let jumping from one position to another upset the swing of the rhythm.

Table of Bass Figures

The following bass figures are the ones most frequently used. Study them as suggested in this chapter. They are usually fingered as indicated. You may finger them as you wish, but keep the fingering consistent.

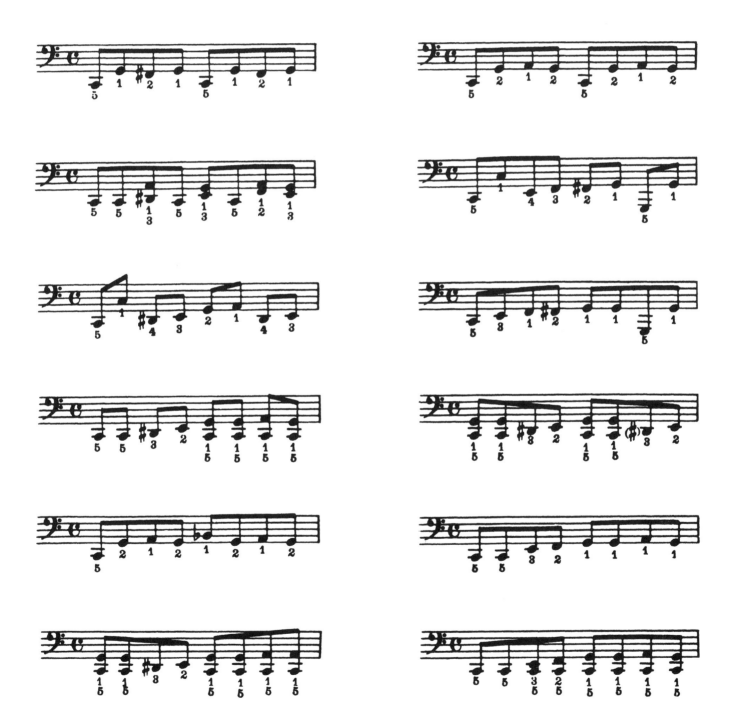

Chapter Four

THE RIGHT HAND

Rhythm and Dynamics

Often the beginner kills any chances of mastering Boogie Woogie by trying to play each note in the right hand with the same force and dynamics as each note in the left hand—as in the following passage.

This method must fail, since it goes against the swing of the right hand by failing to take into account the phrasing and dynamics of the right hand. Note what the right hand is trying to say, its phrasing and dynamics.

The beginner should realize that the right hand has a musical life of its own which cannot be dominated by the left hand. The right hand keeps in "swing" with the left hand, but retains its own personality.

Method

The method for developing the right hand consists in the attempt to build the habit of feeling the exact meaning, dynamics, and rhythm, of each note, and of articulating each note exactly as you feel it. Practice the following right hand figurations according to the phrasing, and dynamics indicated. Articulate exactly and cleanly, so that the passages begin to swing.

Tips on Playing Boogie Woogie Effects

Often in published music, the beginner comes across Boogie Woogie effects which he doesn't know how to translate into sound.

"Crushed" Notes

(1) "Crushed" note to a chord

If you are not playing it satisfactorily, try to make it sound like this:

To play the effect as suggested use one stroke and use the same finger.

(2) "Crushed" note to a single note

This passage originally sounds like this:

To gain the effect—play the "crushed" note as close as possible to the note it decorates with the same finger, using one stroke.

Decorations

Remember that the speed and swing of a composition has much to do with the best way to fit in these effects.

Exercises on Boogie Woogie Effects

Don't let the effect upset the rhythm.

Chapter Five

BOTH HANDS

When the beginner masters the following exercises he will be able to play Boogie Woogie with freedom and ease, and with the right "swing". The introductory exercises consist of simple mechanical figures. The Boogie Woogie exercises start with simple Boogie Woogie rhythm figures and wind up with more complicated figures. Added to this the exercises stress the mastering of special Boogie Woogie effects. The exercises purposely do not feature cross-rhythms such as

since the beginner has not enough command and control of the piano to make any progress in Boogie Woogie from such a standpoint; the exercises feature rhythms that "swing" and have a musical meaning for the beginner.

Suggestions

In the introductory exercises:

(1) Do not attempt playing with both hands unless you have mastered a bass figure.

(2) Don't leave an exercise until you have mastered it.

In the Boogie Woogie exercises:

(1) Try to feel the rhythm, swing, and meaning of each note in the right hand.

(2) Work out the right hand separately if the treble figure seems difficult, before playing with both hands.

(3) At all times play with a steady tempo and make the exercises "swing"

Introductory Exercises

Exercise 1

Exercise 2

Exercise 3

Boogie Woogie Exercises

Exercise 1

Exercise 2

Exercise   3

Exercise 4

Exercise 5

Exercise 6

Exercise 7

Exercise 8

Exercise 9

Exercise 10

Exercise 11

Exercise 12

Exercise 13

38

Exercise 14

EASY MUSICAL TERMS

(Pronunciation in middle column; the strong syllables underlined. A fairly accurate English spelling may be used for all the Italian vowel sounds except their "E" and "o". We use "AY" for the first but it should not be spoken broadly as in English, but rather, greatly shortened. Likewise, the "OH" should not be drawled; it must be short.)

GENERAL EXPRESSIONS

ASSAI	(AH-SAH-EE)	A great deal
BEN	(BAYN)	Well
CODA (⊕)	(KOH-DAH)	Short added section sometimes used to end a movement or a piece.
CON	(KOHN)	With
DA CAPO (D.C.)	(DAH KAH-POH)	Return to beginning and repeat.
DAL SEGNO (D.S.) (𝄋)	(DAHL SAYN-YOH)	Return to sign and repeat.
E (BEFORE VOWEL, ED)	(AY), (AYD)	And
FERMATA (⌒)	(FAYR-MAH-TAH)	Hold
FINE	(FEE-NAY)	The end
GLISSANDO (GLISS.)	(GLEE-SAHN-DOH)	Slide through the notes.
MOLTO	(MOHL-TOH)	Very much
NON	(NOHN)	Not
OPUS (OP.)	(OH-PUS)	A published composition
OTTAVA (8VA)	(OH-TAH-VAH)	Play octave higher or lower, depending on position of sign over or under the notes.
POCO A POCO	(POH-KOH AH POH-KOH)	Little by little
PRIMO (1°)	(PREE-MOH)	First, as in Tempo 1°—return to first speed.
SCHERZO	(SKAYR-TSOH)	A playful piece
SEMPRE	(SAYM-PRAY)	Always
SENZA	(SAYN-DZAH)	Without
SIMILE (SIM.)	(SEE-MEE-LAY)	The same
TENUTO (TEN.)	(TAY-NOO-TOH)	Hold
TROPPO	(TROH-POH)	Too much

EXPRESSIONS OF LOUDNESS AND SOFTNESS

CRESCENDO (CRESC.<)	(KRAY-SHAYN-DOH)	Gradually louder
DIMINUENDO (DIM.>)	(DEE-MEE-NOO-AYN-DOH)	Gradually softer
FORTE (f)	(FOHR-TAY)	Loud
FORTISSIMO (ff)	(FOHR-TEE-SEE-MOH)	Very loud
MARCATO (MARC.)	(MAHR-KAH-TOH)	Emphasize the tone
MEZZO	(MAY-TSOH)	Medium
MEZZO FORTE (mf)		Medium loud
MEZZO PIANO (mp)		Medium soft
MORENDO	(MOH-RAYN-DOH)	Dying away
PIANO (p)	(PEE-AH-NOH)	Soft
PIANISSIMO (pp)	(PEE-AH-NEE-SEE-MOH)	Very soft
SFORZANDO (sfz)	(SFOHR-TSAHN-DOH)	Sharp accent
TRE CORDE	(TRAY KOHR-DAY)	Used after Una Corda to show soft pedal no longer needed.
UNA CORDA	(OO-NAH KOHR-DAH)	Soft pedal

EXPRESSIONS OF SPEED

ACCELERANDO (ACCEL.)	(AH-CHAY-LAY-RAHN-DOH)	Gradually speeding up
ADAGIO	(AH-DAH-JOH)	Very slow

EASY MUSICAL TERMS (*Continued*)

Agitato	(AH-JEE-TAH-TOH)	Agitated, excited
Alla Breve (¢)	(AH-LAH BRAY-VAY)	Half-note is unit of beat; also called cut time.
Allegretto	(AH-LAY-GRAY-TOH)	Medium fast
Allegro	(AH-LAY-GROH)	Fast
Allargando (allarg.)	(AH-LAHR-GAHN-DOH)	Slower and broader
Andante	(AHN-DAHN-TAY)	Medium slow
Andantino	(AHN-DAHN-TEE-NOH)	A bit faster than Andante
A tempo	(AH TAYM-POH)	In time
Grave	(GRAH-VAY)	Slow and dignified
Larghetto	(LAHR-GAY-TOH)	Fairly slow and broad
Largo	(LAHR-GOH)	Very slow and broad
Lento	(LAYN-TOH)	Slow
Meno	(MAY-NOH)	Less
Moderato (mod.)	(MOH-DAY-RAH-TOH)	Medium speed
Più	(PEE-OO)	More
Presto	(PRAY-STOH)	Very fast
Rallentando (rall.)	(RAH-LAYN-TAHN-DOH)	Gradually slower; usually used before change of tempo or at end of piece.
Ritardando (rit.)	(REE-TAHR-DAHN-DOH)	Same as rall. But used elsewhere in piece.
Ritenuto (rit.)	(REE-TAY-NOO-TOH)	Same as above
Stringendo (string.)	(STREEN-JAYN-DOH)	Faster
Tempo Primo (1°)	(TAYM-POH PREE-MOH)	Original speed; used after a slow-down or speed-up to show return to first speed.
Vivace (viv.)	(VEE-VAH-CHAY)	Lively

EXPRESSIONS OF STYLE

Ad Libitum (ad lib.)	(AHD LEE-BEE-TOOM)	At liberty; as you wish
Animato	(AH-NEE-MAH-TOH)	Lively
Brillante	(BREE-LAHN-TAY)	With brilliance
Cantabile	(KAHN-TAH-BEE-LAY)	In a singing manner
Con Grazia	(KOHN GRAH-TSEE-AH)	With grace
Con Moto	(KOHN MOH-TOH)	Move along
Dolce	(DOHL-CHAY)	Gently
Energico	(AY-NAYR-JEE-KOH)	With energy
Espressivo (esp.)	(AY-SPRAY-SEE-VOH)	With feeling
Giocoso	(JOH-KOH-ZOH)	Playfully
Giusto	(JOO-STOH)	Strict
Grandioso	(GRAHN-DEE-OH-ZOH)	Grandly
Grazioso	(GRAH-TSEE-OH-ZOH)	Gracefully
Lamentoso	(LAH-MAYN-TOH-ZOH)	Mournfully
Legato (leg.)	(LAY-GAH-TOH)	One key not released until next key is pressed down.
Leggiero (legg.)	(LAY-JAY-ROH)	Lightly
Maestoso	(MAH-AYS-TOH-ZOH)	With majesty
Misterioso	(MEE-STAY-REE-OH-ZOH)	Mysteriously
Passionato	(PAH-SHOH-NAH-TOH)	With fire
Pedale (ped.)(⎵)	(PAY-DAH-LAY)	Damper (loud) pedal
Perdendo	(PAYR-DAYN-DOH)	Dying away
Pesante	(PAY-ZAHN-TAY)	Heavy
Risoluto	(REE-ZOH-LOO-TOH)	Firmly and strongly
Ritmico	(REET-MEE-KOH)	Rhythmically
Rubato	(ROO-BAH-TOH)	Slowing down some of the melody notes and speeding up others to make up the lost time.
Scherzando	(SKAYR-TSAHN-DOH)	Playfully
Sostenuto (sost.)	(SOH-STAY-NOO-TOH)	In a slowing down and very legato manner.
Staccato	(STAH-KAH-TOH)	The key struck shortly
Triste	(TREE-STAY)	Sadly

Answer To The Prayer

By MEADE "LUX" LEWIS, MARGARET COLEMAN
and BISHOP EDSEL AMMONS

Medium Boogie Tempo

© Johnson

Down The Road A Piece

Words and Music by
DON RAYE

46

48

F Optional Chorus

Coda

* *If the beginner finds section F too difficult he may omit it and jump from ✠ in section E to ✠ in section F*